Henry Goodwin Smith

The History of the Old Scots Church

of Freehold

Henry Goodwin Smith

The History of the Old Scots Church
of Freehold

ISBN/EAN: 9783337410094

Printed in Europe, USA, Canada, Australia, Japan

Cover: Foto ©ninafisch / pixelio.de

More available books at **www.hansebooks.com**

THE HISTORY

OF

THE "OLD SCOTS" CHURCH

OF FREEHOLD

FROM THE SCOTCH IMMIGRATION OF 1685 TILL THE REMOVAL OF THE CHURCH UNDER THE MINISTRY OF THE REV. WILLIAM TENNENT, JR.

BY HENRY GOODWIN SMITH,
Minister of the Freehold Church.

FREEHOLD, N. J.
TRANSCRIPT PRINTING HOUSE
1895.

CONTENTS.

                                                                                     PAGE.

THE SCOTCH IMMIGRATION OF 1685.   5-12

    The Condition in France. In England. In Scotland. Argyle's Revolt. Persecutions of the Summer. Lord Neil Campbell's Expedition. Pitlochie and the "Henry and Francis." The Settlement in Monmouth County.

THE EARLY DAYS OF THE CHURCH   13-18

    The Site. The Graves. The Accepted Date, 1692. The County Record of 1705. The Apprehension of Opposition from Cornbury and Morris. The Qualifying of John Boyd.

THE FIRST PRESBYTERY MEETING.   19-23

    The First Page of the Minutes. The Beginning of American Presbyterian Church History. McKemie. Andrews. Hampton. No Elders Present. The Ordination.

REV. JOHN BOYD, 1706-1708   24-29

    His Past. His Ministry Prior to Ordination. His Examination. His Ordination. His Three Overtures in Presbytery. His Mission Work. Contemporaneous Events. His Tombstone. Its Inscription. Its Condition. Its Proper Preservation.

REV. JOSEPH MORGAN, 1709-1729   30-38

    His Early Life and Prior Settlements. His Qualifying. His Connection With the Dutch Church. With the Presbytery. His Inventions. His Publications. His Tract on Church Unity. The Charges Against Him. Missionary Activity. His Later Life.

REV. JOHN TENNENT, 1730-1732   39-47

    His Early Life, Conversion, Training, Licensure. Condition of The Freehold Church. Walter Ker's Effort. The Ordination. His Ministry and Success. His Death. His Tombstone. His Writings. Summary of His Life.

THE REMOVAL OF THE CHURCH.   48-52

    Reasons for the Removal. Fear of Division. Change in Location of Settlers. Decay of The "Old Scots" Meeting-House. William Tennent, Jr. John Woodhull, D. D. Walter Ker's Grave.

APPENDIX.

CHAPTER I.

THE SCOTCH IMMIGRATION OF 1685.

The Condition in France. In England. In Scotland. Argyle's Revolt. Persecutions of the Summer. Lord Neil Campbell's Expedition. Pitlochie and the "Henry and Francis." The Settlement in Monmouth County.

At no time since the days of Calvin and of Knox was the outlook for the Reformed faith darker in Great Britain and France than in the year 1685. In that year Louis XIV. was persuaded to revoke the Edict of Nantes, which for over eighty years had been the shield of toleration for the Protestantism of France. Six hundred thousand Huguenots sought exile, fleeing from the persecutions of the "dragonnades," and enriched Holland, England and America with the industry, character, and faith which a century later proved to be the sorest needs of the land from which they had been so ruthlessly expelled.

Early in the year, on the death of his brother Charles, James II. ascended the throne of Great Britain, and in defiance of the past opposition to his succession on account of his Romanist views, openly avowed himself a Catholic. The ritual of the Roman church was celebrated at Westminster in Holy Week, the court soon assumed a papist complexion, the Capital silently acquiesced, but in the West of England and in Scotland discontent ripened in a few weeks into revolt. Had leaders appeared with characters and reputations that would have fairly represented the Protestant sentiment of the land, the revolution might well have been anticipated, which three years later brought William of Orange to the English throne. But Duke Monmouth, the vain, luxurious, natural son of Charles II., strove in vain to rally the pure, stern piety of England and of Scotland to the blue banner of his Protestant uprising in the West, and died as a traitor to the King's person and the "King's religion," which gained a passing strength by the failure of this so-called "Protestant rebellion."

The Scottish contingent of Monmouth's revolt was led by the Earl of Argyle. Landing his forces in May on the coast of Cantyre, he endeavored to win to the venturous cause the persecuted Presbyterian element of Western Scotland. The cautious Scotchmen doubted the right of Monmouth's claims to the throne, they disliked his volatile character, and they had not forgotten his part in the slaughter of their brethren at Bothwell Bridge. They remembered also Argyle's "moderate" policy in the past, and his vote in Council, which but four years before sealed the fate of the martyred Cargill.

The cross of blazing yew, quenched in goat's blood, sent as the ancient war-summons through the glens of Argyleshire, was obeyed by only a portion of the great clan of the Campbells.

The harryings and slaughters of the long cruel years of Charles II. had broken the strength of Scotland's Covenant; the noblest of her leaders were imprisoned, exiled, or preparing to fly to the colonies, and the heads of this movement, Monmouth and Argyle, brought no assurance of help to the Covenant. The faint-hearted band of insurgents dispersed at the first opposition, and Argyle was beheaded in Edinburgh in June, two weeks before Monmouth's death in the Tower.

That summer of 1685 witnessed the "bloody circuit" in West England, when the ferocious Jeffreys hung or exiled a thousand for participating in Monmouth's cause. In Scotland, Claverhouse raided the districts of Dumfries and Galloway, making the abjuration of the Covenant the alternative to imprisonment or death. In the month of May, Margaret Wilson and Margaret McLaughlan were drowned in the tidewaters of Blednock, singing their psalms of praise until the waters sealed their lips.[1] Burnt Island prison and Dunnottar Castle heard the piteous prayers of hundreds of suffering Presbyterians, who refused to renounce their allegiance to Christ as the Head of His people.

Macaulay [History, i., 504, 5] says that "Through many years the autumn of 1685 was remembered as a time of misery and terror." "Never, not even under the tyranny of Laud, had the condition of the Puritans been more deplorable than at that time."

Out from this blackness of darkness that enveloped Scotland, the Covenanters looked westward for deliverance and light. Tidings of the free life of some of the colonies where toleration of religion was observed came to them as a bright vision to those that dream. The chartered provisions for religious freedom in the colony of East Jersey attracted them especially to that portion of the new continent. The interest in the proprietory rights of the colony held by many prominent and excellent Scotchmen gave added inducements for emigration thither. The harbor of Leith was alive with the parties of Quakers and Covenanters who turned their stern, saddened faces westward in faith and hope and prayer.

After Argyle's death many of the clan of the Campbells were hung or sentenced to be deported to the colonies. Hearing the threats of the Council to exterminate the clan, Lord Neil Campbell, brother of the unfortunate earl, purchased a proprietory right in the colony of East Jersey, and in the autumn of the year fled to America, leading over several scores of adherents of his brother's cause and of the persecuted faith. He was received with marks of distinction by the East Jersey proprietors upon the field, and in the following year was appointed Deputy Governor of the province. In the quaint chirography of James Emott, of Amboy, clerk of the province, is the list of Campbell's emigrants of 1685, and among their number we may find names of those who, a few years after, reared the Church of their Covenanted faith on "Free hill" in the county of Monmouth.[2]

Toward the close of the year there arrived at Perth Amboy the "Henry and Francis," a vessel "of 350 tun and 20 great guns," the pest ship containing the stricken remnant of the sad expedition organized by George Scot, laird of Pitlochie. Few pages of history are fuller of mingled misery, horror and moral grandeur, than the records of these persecuted followers of Pitlochie. Sentenced to death for attending conventicles and refusing allegiance to the Papist James, they were lying in the summer of 1685, tortured and mutilated, in the prisons of Glasgow and Edinburgh, Stirling and Leith. Pitlochie, who had been fined enormous sums and thrice imprisoned for his Presbyterian principles, obtained for them a commutation of sentence to banishment for life. Collecting from the stifling dungeons this wretched crowd of men and women, with ears cropped, and noses slit, and cheeks branded, he embarked with them in September only to lose his life upon the passage, his wife and some seventy of his fellow-sufferers also perishing from the pestilent ship-fever. On this voyage of horrors, with the memory of persecution and tyranny behind them, with the plague carrying away three and four from their number daily, with the hardships of the untried wilderness before them, their indomitable spirits rose above all these miseries that encompassed them and they sent back to Scotland the protest against the injustice that banished them from their "own native and covenanted land, by an unjust sentence, for owning truth, and holding by duty, and studying to keep by their covenanted engagements and baptismal vows, whereby they stand obliged to resist, and testify against all that is contrary to the word of God and their covenants." Concerning their attitude toward King James they say "their sentence of banishment ran chiefly because they refused the oath of allegiance, which in conscience they could not take, because in so doing, they thought they utterly declined the Lord Jesus Christ from having any power in his own house, and practically would by taking it, say he was not King and head of his church and over their consciences; and on the contrary, this was to take and put in his room a man whose breath is in his nostrils, yea, a man that is a sworn enemy to religion, an avowed papist, whom by our covenant we are bound to withstand and disown." [Wodrow, History, iv., pp. 331, 332.] This declaration of allegiance to the supremacy of spiritual truth over all earthly powers, rings in our ears like the challenge of a trumpet peal; clear, strident, and inspiring.

Their sufferings were intensified by the inhuman treatment received upon the voyage. "When they who were under deck attempted to worship God by themselves the captain would throw down great planks in order to disturb them." The captain also proposed taking the wretched cargo to Virginia or Jamaica and offered to dispose of them "in bulk."

Wodrow states that the emigrants found but inhospitable treatment from "the people who lived on the coast side" but received many acts of kindness from the inhabitants of a town "a little way up the country." This place of their first sojourn was probably Woodbridge, where the sufferers found a Puritan settlement of New Englanders. Many of them came over to Monmouth county, after litigation with John Johnstone, Pitlochie's son-in-law, on whom the command of the expedition devolved at the leader's death. Mr. Johnstone, according to Wodrow's account, sued many of them as "Redemptioners" for four years service, according to the agreement in Scot's "Model" for those who went over without remuneration. As seventy-two of the passengers were said to be "presents to the Laird" being "prisoners banished to the plantations" the demand does not seem an unjust one. Johnstone obtained a plantation in Monmouth named "Scotschesterburg," and rose to prominence as a political leader of the "Scotch" party in the colony.

Although these two expeditions of 1685 were the most notable of those days they were not the first or only organized parties of Scotch immigrants. In the year 1682, the twenty-four proprietors, a number of whom were Scotchmen, on coming into possession of the soil of East Jersey, offered many inducements to settle in the new colony. Among those who came over in this first year of general immigration, we find the names of William and Margaret Redford, born in the years 1642 and 1645, who lie buried in the "Old Scots" graveyard,

The Tombstone of the Oldest Covenanters Buried in the "Old Scots" Ground, who Came in the First Year of Scotch Immigration.

under a double stone, reproduced in the accompanying cut. The years of their respective births are the oldest recorded in the grave-yard.

In 1684, Scot of Pitlochie published his " Model of the Government of East Jersey in America," showing its advantages as a " retreat where, by law, a toleration is allowed * * * * no where else to be found in his majesty's dominions." Barclay of Ury, the grand old Quaker Governor of the colony, together with Lawrie and Drummond, his Deputies on the field, with motives of mingled compassion and business interest, organized many parties of harassed Scotch Quakers and Covenanters, who on their arrival at Perth Amboy, the port of the colony, soon found their way to the broad plains of Middlesex and Monmouth counties.[3]

The famous emigrant ship, the " Caledonia,"[4] is supposed to have made her first voyages at this early period, and other well-known Covenanters, such as Walter Ker,[5] pillar of the Freehold Church for half a century, are known to have come in the year 1685.

On entering Monmouth county, the Presbyterian Immigrants found the neighborhood of the Navesink neck already in the possession of the Monmouth patent men, among whom at first the Baptist element predominated. The Shrewsbury settlement was largely of Quakers, many of whom were brought to the established church through the agency of the persuasive and energetic George Keith. The Covenanters would naturally seek a locality where they might form a community of their own and might dwell together in fellowship. Some of them settled near the present town of Matawan, where before the year 1690 was a hamlet known as New Aberdeen.[6] The larger portion of them advanced somewhat farther into the interior and in the large district known then as Freehold found peace and plenteousness after their sufferings and wanderings. Freehold obtained its first character as a community from the Covenanter immigrants of 1682-1685.[7]

"This is the era at which East Jersey, till now chiefly colonized from New England, became the asylum of Scottish Presbyterians," says Bancroft, [Colonial History, chap. xvii.] "Is it strange," he continues, "that Scottish Presbyterians of virtue, education and courage, blending a love of popular liberty with religious enthusiasm, hurried to East Jersey in such numbers as to give to the rising commonwealth a character which a century and a half has not effaced." "Thus the mixed character of New Jersey springs from the different sources of its people. Puritans, Covenanters, and Quakers met on her soil; and their faith, institutions, and preferences, having life in the common mind, survive the Stuarts."

CHAPTER II.

THE EARLY DAYS OF THE CHURCH.

The Site. The Graves. The Accepted Date, 1692. The County Record of 1705. The Apprehension of Opposition from Cornbury and Morris. The Qualifying of John Boyd.

Some six miles to the north of the present town of Freehold, on a wooded eminence, overlooking rolling, fertile fields, lies a neglected acre which should be a cherished spot to all Presbyterians of our land, and also to all interested in the beginnings of the colonial history.[8] It is the site of the "Old Scots" Church of Freehold, reared by the exiles of 1685 for their worship of God after the simple manner forbidden in their own "native and covenanted land." The view presented in the accompanying cut shows a portion of this "God's Acre," with the church site in the foreground. Of the building itself, no memory, tradition, or trace remains, except the slight depression in the soil, which would indicate the humble dimensions of a structure perhaps some twenty feet square.[9] Close under its eaves were laid the remains of its first minister, Rev. John Boyd. Eight yards to the southwest, under a horizontal stone that is sinking in the turf, lies the body of Rev. John Tennent, who, like Rev. John Boyd, died in his youth after two years of ministry with the church.

Around this central site lie the rude stones of the old Scotch pilgrims and their children, of Archibald Craige, one of Lord Campbell's company, of John Henderson, son probably of him of the same name who signed the protest on Pitlochie's ship, of Formans of the generation following John Foreman of the "Henry and Francis," and others of the names of Clark, Redford, Wall and Ward, belonging to the Covenanter generation, others still of the names of Amy. Crawford, O'Harrah, Pease, Patten, VanDorn, and Freeiser of the generation of the sons and daughters born in the new world.[10]

The generally accepted date for the erection of the church building, or the organization of the church society, is the year 1692.[11] The only basis apart from tradition appears to be a Mss. letter from Freehold by Rev. John Woodhull, D. D., dated April 23rd, 1792, which stated that "The Church was formed about an hundred years ago, chiefly by persons from Scotland." [Hodge's History, i. 56.]

Taking into consideration the tenacity of the Covenanters' religious convictions, and the liberty of worship bought by their exile, it seems improbable that many years could have passed before they assembled in "conventicles," unharassed by fear of dragoon or blood hound, sword or gibbet. The strenuous labor of reclaiming the soil to productiveness would not turn those worthies of faith from confessing that they were pilgrims and sojourners seeking the better and heavenly country, and in their assembling themselves together, after the plain customs of the church of Knox, these loyal Scotchmen would find both their clearest duty and their highest joy. It would be at variance with their character and circumstances to suppose a later date than 1692 for the beginning of the little kirk, the appointment of elders or "assistants," and the rearing of the building, made of logs or rough-hewn timbers. For a period of fourteen years without a settled minister to conduct the services and administer the sacraments, the neighboring Covenanters doubtless gathered upon the Lord's day, read the Scriptures, sang their metrical versions of David's Psalms, catechized the children, and joined in prayer led by John Craig or Walter Ker or John Henderson, adoring the God of Deliverance for their escapes from perils and tribulations, and invoking the continuance of his covenant of grace to their children and to generations yet unborn.[12]

The Scotchmen would be joined in these services by some of their fellow Presbyterians from Holland and from France, who came to the region in the later years of the century, and formed strong affiliations with the Scotch, uniting in fullest sympathy with their Calvinistic doctrines and in fellowship in sufferings. The names of DuBois, La Rue, shortened to Rue, and Perrin, or Perrine, indicate the Huguenot parentage of some of the early settlers. Concerning the Dutch immigration more will be said in the chapter on Rev. Joseph Morgan, who was pastor of both the Scotch and Dutch churches of Freehold.

The first authentic statement concerning the early history of the church is contained in the early records of the courts of the County of Monmouth.

This is the action taken by four representative Presbyterians in the county who desired the " recording " of their Meeting-house by the court. A fac-simile of this request, of the consequent action of the court, and of the application of the Rev. John Boyd for leave to " qualify " is given.

The record reads as follows:—At a Court held on Fourth Tuesday of December 1705. John Bowne, President.

Richard Salter, Obadiah Bowne, Anthony Woodward, George Allen, Jeremiah Stillwell, Assistants.

At ye request of John Craig, Walter Ker, William Bennet, Patrick Imly, in behalf of themselves and their breathren, ye protestant desenters of freehold called Presbiterians, that their Publick meeting house may be recorded. Ordered by this Cort, that it be Recorded as followeth. The Meeting House for religious worship, belonging to the Protistant discenters, called ye Presbiterians of ye Town of Freehold, in ye County of Monmouth, in ye Province of New Jarsey, is scituate, built, lying and being at and upon a piece of Rising grownd, commonly known and called by the name of free hill in sd Town.

Mr. John Boyd, Minnister of the sd Presbiterians of freehold, did also Parsonally appear, and did desire that he might be admitted to qualify himself, as the law directs in that behalf.

Ordered that further consideration thereof be referred until the next Court of Quarter Sessions."

The reason for the "Recording" of the church property may well have been an apprehension of some act of injustice or extortion on the part of Lord Cornbury who was then governor of New Jersey and New York. His administration of affairs in New York was disgraced by a series of illegal acts toward dissenting churches and ministers. In New York City, in Westchester county, and on Long Island, Puritan church buildings were turned over to the established church, and both ministers and congregations were forced to conform or to retire.

Although there was no establishment of the Episcopal church in the Jersies, to give color to any similar

The Earliest Official Record of the "Old Scots" Church and John Boyd.
From the Monmouth County Records of the Court Held
on the Fourth Tuesday in December, 1705.

action. the cautious Scotchmen wished to avail themselves of every safe-guard.[13]

The spreading upon the court records of the position of the meeting house, and the acknowledgement by the legal authorities that it was the property of " ye desenters called ye Presbiterians " gave a certain legal security of title, being an endorsement by the constituted authorities of their ownership and their rights to own.

Assuming the church to have been in existence since 1692, a reason why thirteen years elapsed before making the record, may be found in the fact that up to the year 1704 the court of the county had been, almost without interruption, under the power of Lewis Morris, a zealous churchman, who showed his ecclesiastical preferences, however, more in bitter opposition to dissent than in any earnest efforts to propagate Episcopacy. In the year 1704, the county courts fell into the hands of the Patent men of Middletown, many of whom were Baptists. The Presbyterians, therefore, took the earliest occasion practicable to secure from their fellow-dissenters upon the bench the legal recognition of their possessions.

The zeal and success with which George Keith had in the last few years been leading the Quakers of Shrewsbury and Freehold into the communion of the established church, was an added cause for alarm and for energetic action on the part of the Presbyterians, who remembered that Keith had begun his varied ecclesiastical career in the Kirk of Scotland.

The appearance of the young minister, Rev. John Boyd, at the same court sessions was another act of precaution to preserve the person of the preacher from the outrages and tyranny of the Governor. Cornbury's treatment of Morgan of Eastchester [who was Boyd's successor at Freehold,] of Hubbard of Jamaica, of McKemie and Hampton when preaching at Newton, and even of Episcopalian ministers in New Jersey who fell under his displeasure[11] gave abundant warrant for taking every step to ensure safety from the attacks of the man who, Bancroft says, "joined the worst form of arrogance to intellectual imbecility." [Hist. of U. S. ii. p. 41.]

The court, in December, 1705, deferred action upon Rev. John Boyd's request until the following May. Inasmuch as they had no action in a similar case to guide them as precedent, and as most of the judges on the bench were unfamiliar with judicial duties, the court probably felt unwilling and unable immediately to decide the rather intricate question of the status of a dissenting minister in the province, without opportunity for consultation, and possibly for reference to authorities in England for advice.

In May, 1706, Mr. Boyd appearing again before them, he was permitted to "qualify" by subscribing to the provisions of three acts, made in the reigns of Elizabeth, Charles II., and William and Mary, which contained an abjuration of Transubstantiation, an assent to the doctrine of the Trinity as taught in the xxxix Articles and the Oaths of Allegiance and Supremacy;[15] all being contained in the Toleration Act of 1689, which freed dissenting ministers from the obnoxious restrictions of the Five Mile Act and Conventicle Act.

CHAPTER III.

THE FIRST PRESBYTERY MEETING.

The First Page of the Minutes. The Beginning of American Presbyterian Church History. McKemie. Andrews. Hampton. No Elders Present. The Ordination.

"De Regimine ecclesiæ." Concerning the government of the church—with these striking and characteristic words, in the midst of a broken sentence, the history of the Presbyterian church in America begins. This incomplete phrase ushers us into the midst of an interesting scene. The place is the "Old Scots" church of Freehold, or some spot near it, the day is Friday, December 27th, 1706. The revered Francis McKemie, "Father of the American Presbyterian Church," is occupying with appropriateness the Moderator's chair, the other ministers present are Jedediah Andrews of Philadelphia, and John Hampton of Maryland, and the Presbyterial action is the examination of Rev. John Boyd, with a view to his ordination to the gospel ministry and his connection with the Freehold church.

A reproduction of this first page of the minutes of the Presbytery of Philadelphia is given herewith.

"1706. De Regimine ecclesiæ, which being heard was approved of and sustained. He gave in also his thesis to be considered of against next sederunt.

Sederunt 2d, 10bris, 27.

Post preces sederunt, Mr. Francis McKemie, Moderator, Messrs. Jedidiah Andrews and John Hampton, Ministers.

Mr. John Boyd performed the other parts of his tryals, viz. preached a popular sermon on John i. 12; defended his thesis; gave satisfaction as to his skill in the Languages, and answered to extemporary questions; all which were approved of and sustained.

Appointed his ordination to be on ye next Lord's day, ye 29th inst., which was accordingly performed in the publick meeting house of this place, before a numerous assembly; and the next day he had ye Certificat of his ordination."

This memorable scene is the beginning of organic Presbyterian history in the new world. This is the first known Presbytery meeting, and the first known Presbyterian ordination. There may have been Presbytery meetings and ordinations prior to this. There probably were ordinations before this, and ordinations presuppose a Presbytery to ordain.[16] Yet in tracing back to its sources the wondrous course of the development of the church, history stops at John Boyd, and the "Old Scots" meeting house of Freehold. Back of this point lie the uncertainties of tradition or conjecture. Onward from this, all is clear, cogent and connected. From the threshold of the little meeting house on Free Hill began the tiny current of the stream, which, as in the prophet's vision, has spread through distant deserts, deepening in its progress, watering thirsty places, and bringing its nourishment to the trees of life.

All of the men appearing in this scene are well-known. Francis McKemie, the apostle of Presbyterianism, founder of half a dozen churches in Maryland, energetic, practical, determined, devout, the embodiment of the Scotch-Irish character, presides with fitness over the gathering, for no other man had been more active or successful in fostering the nascent Presbyterianism scattered throughout the land. He was at this time on a trip eastward and three weeks later, after preaching in New York and Newtown, together with Hampton, was arrested by Governor Cornbury on the frivolous

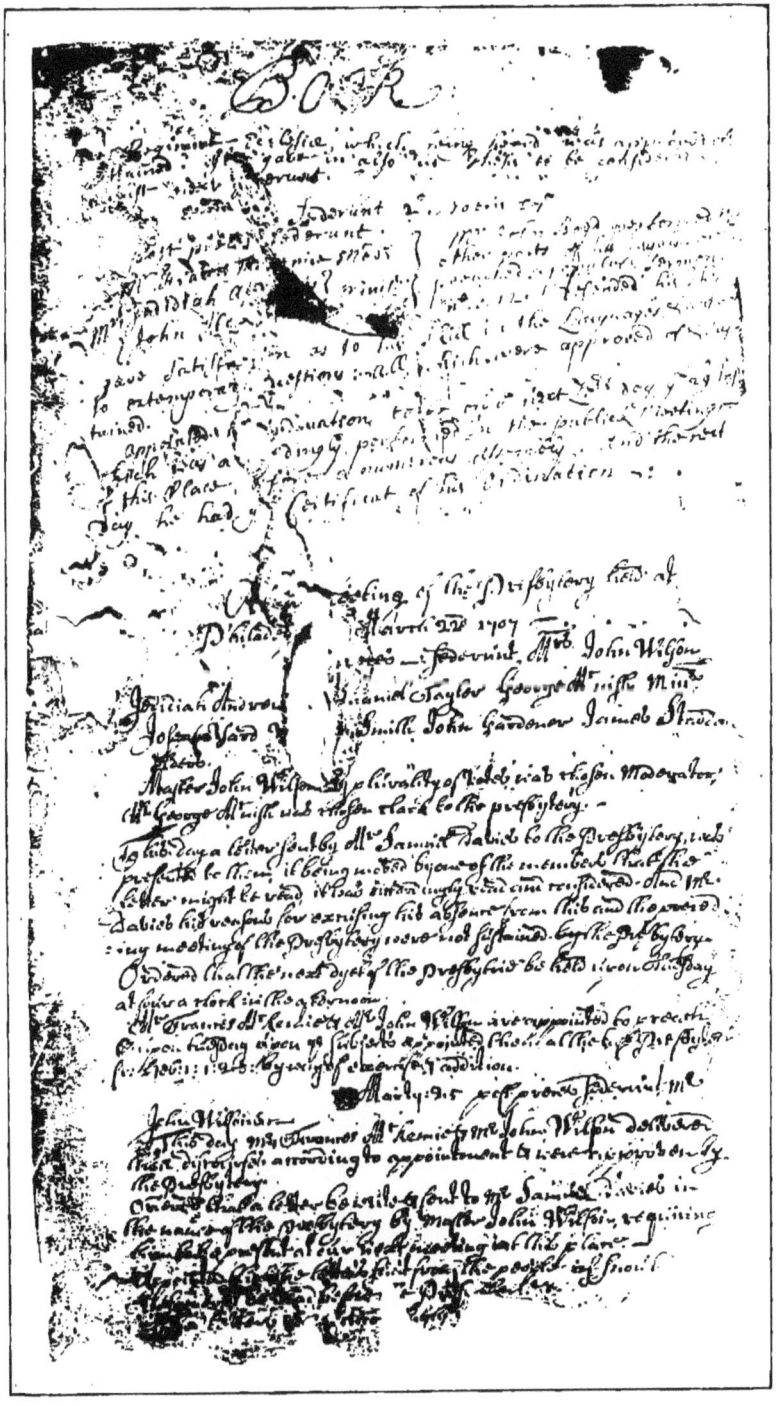

The "First Page" of the Minutes of the Presbytery of Philadelphia: the Account of the Ordination of Rev. John Boyd of Freehold.
[Kindness of Presbyterian Historical Society.]

charge of preaching without the Governor's license. After imprisonment, he was released on bail, and although subsequently acquitted, was unjustly compelled to pay heavy costs. The indignation aroused by this outrage throughout the colonies and in England was one of the many causes determining Cornbury's recall the following year. McKemie died in 1708, "a venerable and imposing character, distinguished for piety, learning, and much steady resolution and perseverance." [Hodge's History, i. 76.]

Jedediah Andrews was the first pastor of the first Presbyterian church of Philadelphia. He was graduated from Harvard College in 1695. He came to Philadelphia in 1698 and took charge of the Presbyterian congregation who had previously worshipped with the Baptists in the "store house on Barbadoes lot." Mr. Andrews attended every recorded meeting of Presbytery and Synod, from this first meeting at Freehold until his death, forty years afterward. He was thrice moderator of the Presbytery and of the Synod of Philadelphia. He was a peace maker in the constitutional debates of 1721 and 1729, a moderate man who neither protested nor signed counter-protests.[17]

John Hampton, the third presbyter present, had come from Ireland in 1705, under McKemie's charge, and supported by the London ministers. He was pastor of the lately organized church at Snowhill, Maryland. It is worthy of notice that McKemie, Hampton and Boyd had all been students at Glasgow University; McKemie in 1675, Hampton in 1696, and Boyd in 1701.[18]

Dr. Hodge, in his History of the Presbyterian Church, [i. 95] notes the fact that this first Presbytery meeting at Freehold is the only one in the records at which no elders sat as members of the body. The lack of a representative of the church with which they were meeting is the more remarkable on account of the excellent and godly men, such as Walter Ker and others, who were in the direction of the spiritual matters of the church.

Upon the following Sabbath, was performed the solemn act of dedicating the life of the young minister to the service of the Church of God. Upon his brow in this symbolic ritual descended the ordination touch of the old world ministry. The new order of the American presbytery was born that day. The difficult question of validity of ordination which brought dissension into other churches, such as the Dutch Presbyterian church of America, was solved in the act. John Boyd heads the long list of Presbyters in the ordination roll of the American Presbyterian Churches.

By the actions on these two days, the Freehold Church became the first recognized Presbyterian Church in New Jersey. "In Jersey, the Church in Freehold was the only one at first belonging to the Presbytery," [Hodge, i. 75.] Abraham Pierson, who was at Newark in 1667, Jeremiah Peck, at Elizabethtown in 1668, Benjamin Salsbury, at Woodbridge in 1674, and Thomas Bridge, at Cohanzy in 1692, all ministered to apparently Independent congregations. The churches at Woodbridge and Cohanzy came into connection with the Presbytery two years later, in 1708,[19] the churches of Maidenhead and Hopewell followed in 1709.[20]

On that last Sabbath day of the year 1706, the Covenanters gathered with gladness, at the sound of the conch shell, or the rolling drum, in their house of religious assembly. One whose services had been approved by over a year of trial, the man of their choice, and of their nation, was to be empowered to exercise his full ministry, and to administer to them the precious sacraments of the Church of Christ. For the first time in the lives of most of them, the exiles of 1685 would now enjoy the full privileges of the church which they had loved and suffered for; privileges which they had been denied by tyrannous intolerance in their native land, and by the undeveloped character of their church life in their new home.

The throngs that would assemble, drawn by deep and prayerful interest in the events, or by the curiosity excited by the wide reputation of Francis McKemie, might not be contained within the narrow walls; and some of those outside the building would pass above the spot where less than two years later rested the ashes of the young Presbyter, who this day was consecrating the ardor of his youth to the service of the Church of Christ.

CHAPTER IV.

REV. JOHN BOYD.

His Past. His Ministry Prior to Ordination. His Examination. His Ordination. His Three Overtures in Presbytery. His Mission Work. Contemporaneous Events. His Tombstone. Its Inscription. Its Condition. Its Proper Preservation.

Concerning the history of the first minister of Freehold, but little is known before his appearance at the County court in 1705.[21] A John Boyd appears on the list of Lord Neil Campbell's expedition of 1685, a time when Boyd of Freehold, from the dates upon his tombstone, was five or six years of age. On March 11, 1701, the name John Boyd is enrolled in the fourth class in Glasgow University, with signs that he was a native of Scotland.[22] The general belief was that the Freehold minister came from Scotland.[23] Webster, [History, p. 90] considers it not unlikely that he came over with McKemie, McNish and Hampton in the autumn of 1705.

Since the Monmouth Court, in December, 1705, termed Boyd "Minnister of ye said Presbiterians," a whole year before he had received ordination at the hands of the Presbytery, and also "qualified" him before he had gained full ecclesiastical standing as a minister, it may be assumed that Mr. Boyd, in proper and orderly manner, had been exercising his function as a licensed preacher, for at least a year in Freehold before the Presbytery meeting of 1706.

Mr. John Boyd's examination for ordination before Presbytery on December 27th, 1706, which included "skill in the languages," a thesis to be defended, a Latin essay " De Regimine ecclesiae," and a popular sermon, indicate an academic and university training, corroborating the view that he had been a student at Glasgow University. The chosen text for his sermon was John 1: 12, " But as many as received him, to them gave he power to become the sons of God, even to them that believe on his name." This is one of those texts that Luther aptly names " little Bibles," and in it the young preacher, before his stern but kindly critics, could manifest his ability to expound, defend and apply the great doctrines of Election, Adoption, Faith and Conversion.

His ordination, on the following Lord's day, did not lead to his installation as pastor of the Freehold church. There is also no record of the installation of his successor in the ministry at Freehold, and that the act of installation was not then universally observed is seen in the fact that William Tennent, Sr., in 1736, is found in the minutes of Synod not to have been installed over the Neshaminy church, with whom he had lived for ten years; the Synod declaring that " he is still to be esteemed as the pastor of that people, notwithstanding the want of a formal installment among them."

Mr. Boyd became an active and efficient member of the Presbytery, for the following year, 1707, in the meeting at Philadelphia, although his name is omitted from the list of those present, he is appointed, with Rev. Jedediah Andrews, to " prepare some overtures to be considered by the Presbytery, for propagating religion in their respective congregations." On the next day the overtures are presented and agreed upon. They are as follows:

"First: That every minister in their respective congregations, read and comment upon a chapter of the Bible every Lord's day, as discretion and circumstances of time, place, etc., will admit."

The hand of Mr. Boyd may be seen in this first overture for the reason that in the following year, Mr. Andrews is mentioned by name as not having complied with the provisions.

"Second over : That it be recommended to every minister of the Presbytery to set on foot and encourage private Christian societies."

The bearing and significance of this injunction is not clear. It would appear as prophetic of the multitudes of Leagues, and Young People's Societies, and Mission organizations and Bands, Brotherhoods and Clubs, which are buzzing so actively in the machinery of the modern church, the

"Wheels within wheels
With living creatures wedded."

The third overture relates to the aggressive work of Home Missions, Synodical or local.

"Third over.: That every minister of the Presbytery supply neighbouring desolate places where a minister is wanting, and opportunity of doing good offers."

The spirit of John Boyd is in this recommendation also, for along with his Presbyterial appointment at Cohanzy, in West Jersey, participating in an ordination service, he was also directed, with the consent of his Freehold congregation, to proceed every third week to Woodbridge, where the Scottish portion of the congregation, apparently in antagonism with the older New England settlers, might profit by his sympathy and advice.

Like his successor, Morgan, Mr. Boyd probably preached in various parts of Monmouth county, besides the meeting house upon Free Hill. At Middletown[24] and Shrewsbury, in the neighborhood of the present

Tennent church, and in the regions of Allentown, or Crosswicks, he found opportunity to proclaim the faithful message of his Master, sowing the first seeds of the Gospel upon soil that still bears fruit of his ardent and unrecorded labors.

The twenty short months of his ministry were contemporaneous with the most brilliant portions of the reign of "Good Queen Anne," and Marlborough's successes at Ramillies and Oudenarde were celebrated in the Jersey colonies with loyalty and enthusiasm. The Kingdoms of England and Scotland were united in 1707, and the intensity of feeling between patriots of the two British nationalities, which had been manifested in bitter party spirit in East Jersey, was mitigated and in time removed.

A letter presented by the Freehold people to Presbytery, in 1708, "about the settlement of Mr. Boyd is referred to the next meeting." His premature and apparently sudden death in the summer of that year ends the matter; or, as quaintly expressed in the Presbytery minutes of 1709, "The Rev. Mr. John Boyd being dead, what relates to him ceases."

The tombstone of Mr. Boyd stands in a conspicuous spot in the center of the church grounds, close to the site of the building. It is of brown sandstone, some four feet in height. The stone faces the east, and as the rays of the sun at noon-tide strike across the worn and weather-beaten front, the long Latin inscription, covering the stone to the edges, stands out with characters that are decipherable through most of the sixteen lines.

ENTISSIMI DOMINI JOANNIS
BODIJ CINERES ECCLESIAE HUJUS CAL
VINI PASTOR HIC DEFODIUNTUR
EI OPERAM QUAMVIS STERLI SOLI(?)
CONSUMPTAM NON PERDIDIT
QUI ILLUM PERNOVERUNT AQ
VIRTUTIBUS IN ED(?) INATIS ILLO TE
MPORE DIGNITATEM EIUS EX
PLORAVERUNT LECTOR VESTIG
IA ILLIUS PERSEVERE ET (?)
E(?)EA TEMPORE SPERO MOR
TEM OBIIT TRIGESIMO DIE
AUGUSTI MILLESIMO SEP
TEM CENTESIMO OCTAVO
AETATIS SUAE VICESIMO
NONO

"The ashes of the very pious Rev. John Boyd Pastor of this church of Calvin, are here buried, whose labour, although expended on a sterile soil, was not lost.

They who knew him well also proved his worth as (?) in virtues.

Reader, persevere in his footsteps, and I hope in that time (?)

He died on the thirtieth day of August, one thousand, seven hundred and eight, in the twenty-ninth year of his age."

What relic of the primitive Presbyterianism of the land should be more prized, more jealously guarded, and more reverently preserved than this memorial of the first born of American Presbyterian ministers, who was the first also to fall from the ranks of the ministry, and find burial in the new continent?

In some place of protection from the storms that for well nigh one hundred and ninety years have been striving to efface its significance, in a spot where will be the recognition of its value as a historical and ecclesiastical monument, this weather-beaten, but time-honored stone should rest, and in its place, should stand a

The Tombstone of Rev. John Boyd, First Minister of Freehold. The First Presbyterian Minister Ordained in America.

replica of the original, joined with a suitable and stately memorial of the "First Presbytery Meeting," when the Presbyterianism of the continent first woke to conscious life.

CHAPTER V.

REV. JOSEPH MORGAN.

His Early Life and Prior Settlements. His Qualifying. His Connection With the Dutch Church. With the Presbytery. His Inventions. His Publications. His Tract on Church Unity. The Charges Against Him. Missionary Activity. His Later Life.

The second minister of the Church was the Rev. Joseph Morgan, a man of literary ability and versatile gifts, a ready and prolific writer, whose absorption in mechanical inventions, and in essays on Predestination and Church Unity, followed by periods of spiritual earnestness and fervor, left a mingled and dubious impression upon his strict Scotch congregation. His reputation was lessened by his evident short-comings, and by contrast with the fame of his illustrious successors of the honored name of Tennent.

Rev. Joseph Morgan was born in New London, Conn. November 6, 1674,[25] of stock of which he himself said "that [for Americans] they are a credible family." He was ordained by the Association of Ministers of Fairfield County, Conn. He was at Greenwich in 1696,[26] Bedford in 1700, Eastchester, and Westchester, where, in 1704, he was dispossessed of his charge by Lord Cornbury, who placed Rev. John Bartow, Missionary of the S. P. G., in his place.[27] Mr. Morgan then retired to New England, probably again to Greenwich.

The statement is made, on high authority, that he was one of the graduates of Yale College in the first class that completed a regular course in that institution, in 1702, two years before the college received its corporate powers.[28] President Woolsey wrote that "some interest is attached to Mr. Morgan from the fact that he was not only one of the members of the first class in Yale College, but also the only one who did not also take his degree at Harvard, that is the only one veritably educated at Yale alone."[29]

Mr. Morgan came to Freehold in the latter part of the year 1708, or in 1709. He appeared before the court to qualify in September, 1709, and is then termed " Minister of ye Presbiterians in Freehold and Middletown." Mr. Morgan was " presented by several of said congregation, viz.: Jacob Lane, John Wicof, John Sutfin, William Hendrickson, John Essmith, William Wilkins, and Auri Marbison, in behalf of themselves and the rest of their breathren." The first three of these names were in the communion of the Dutch Reformed Church of Freehold, the other four are said to represent the Presbyterian church.[30] Between Mr. Morgan's application to the court and his qualifying, he was installed on October 17, 1709, as first pastor of the Reformed Church, of Freehold and Middletown, a double congregation of Dutch settlers, sometimes called " the congregation of the Navesink," the second act of installation in the Reformed Church in the Jersies.[31] He was received as a member of the Presbytery of Philadelphia, after debate, in September, 1710. At this meeting the following action is taken:

"It being reported that one Walter Kerr defamed the Presbytery, and Mr. Morgan, minister to said Kerr, desiring advice therein how to behave, it was referred to the said Mr Morgan to take cognizance of the offence, and to act either by private or public censure, as the nature of the thing should appear to him, and that report thereof should be made next meeting."

The differences between Walter Ker and the Presbytery may probably be resolved into differences between Ker and Morgan, for the sturdy consistent old Coven-

anter, with his strict notions of the Church and zeal for
the advancement of his own faith, would probably not
relish the union with the Reformed congregation under
Morgan's ministry, nor would his hard Scotch sense
appreciate many of the eccentric Dominie's schemes and
dreams.

Although Mr. Morgan's ecclesiastical connection from
this time onward was with the Presbytery and Synod of
Philadelphia, he appears to have received more sympathy and more support from the Dutch than from the
Scotch congregation. He occupied the parsonage belonging to the Dutch church with a glebe of "one hundred
acres of good arable land, as good as any in Freehold, on
which a family may subsist comfortably;" and on which
the Dominie seems to have lived comfortably indeed,
realizing from it thirty pounds a year, "besides his own
bread."[32]

Mr. Morgan appeared at the original Presbytery of
Philadelphia only once after his reception in 1710. His
continued absences prompt the Presbytery in 1716 to
direct Jedediah Andrews to write him a letter "informing him that if he comes not, nor sends sufficient
reasons against next year, we shall take it for granted
that he has altogether deserted us." The loss of the
Presbytery minutes of the following year do not allow
us to know the result of this mild warning.

An explanation of his absence from Presbytery during
these years appears in the Archives of New Jersey
for 1714, [1 series, iv., 190-195]. It is a communication from Mr. Morgan to the Lords of Trade concerning a wondrous scheme for the improvement of navigation by an invention, which will work against wind
at sea, will save many a ship from ship-wreck, will

shorten voyages by many weeks and months, and be excellent in war. This prophecy of the days of steam, and ocean grey-hounds, consists in a combination of wheels, cranks, booms, and oars, "Found out in ye year 1712 [to 1714] by Joseph Morgan of Freehold in New Jersey in North America." There follows a description of thirteen modes of applying the invention to ships so that "if any one of these thirteen ways be good my art is good, although twelve of ye ways were good for nothing." Beside his experiments exhibited before "The Governour and Assembly and City of New York" [on June 17th, 1714,] and his writing to "ye Governour of Boston with ye same desire" his brain was occupied with "another art (hitherto unknown to the world) of far (yea an hundred times) greater consequence and benefit to the world," an art unfortunately still unrevealed. He published in the same year a treatise on Baptism, reviewing the "Portsmouth disputation examined." If we add his quiet practice of astrology, it is little wonder that, as he confessed to Cotton Mather, a few years later, "he had no leisure for reading, nor for writing discourses for the church, and often knew not my text before the Sabbath."

Mr. Morgan published a number of his writings. A sermon preached at his own ordination, and also at the ordination of Jonathan Dickinson, at Elizabethtown, Sept. 29th, 1709, was published in New York in 1712.[33] The next year came his treatise on Baptism;[34] he sent to Mather a treatise against the Deists; then followed "A Remedy for mortal errors, showing the necessity for the Anointing of the Spirit"; in 1724 he published a "Reply to an anonymous Railer against the doctrine of Election." He tells Mather he hopes this Book will remove the prejudices "which half the country here away, and almost the other half too, have against our Confession of faith." His orthodoxy is unquestioned, for "of all the agencies Satan has formed against our Salvation, the most effectual is Arminianism." It is to be feared that in this treatise his statements in regard to the divisive doctrine of Christendom were not couched in such conciliatory mode as in a previous work which he sent in 1718 to the S. P. G., the Missionary Society of the English Established Church, on "The most effectual Way to Propagate the Gospel;" for he declares that in this work his unfolding of the doctrine of Predestination was approved both by keen opponents of the doctrine and by strong Predestinarians, "which is a circumstance to hope that it is a platform [as the author proposes] to reconcile the grievous contentions by which the Church is rent to pieces and laid to the mercy of ye adversary."

But apparently he received no more commendation from the authorities of the Established Church than he had from his own Presbyterian brethren, who as he naively confesses, told him that his language was too mean for him to be capable to be a writer of books, and also informed him, "which allmost broke his heart," that his hypothesis was not true! His hypothesis being the unity of the church.[35]

This action of his in making overtures of reconciliation to the Episcopal church would probably not endear him to the Scotch, who had been taught by bitterest experience to identify Prelacy with all that was tyrannical and unjust. It would also rouse the ire of the sturdy Dutch Dominies; and Theodorus Jacobus Frelinghuysen of Raritan, the most prominent Reformed minister in the central portion of the State, accordingly denounced Morgan as the "friend and advocate of a lifeless, God-dishonouring formalism." Possibly the fact that Morgan was willing to baptize the children of disaffected members of Frelinghuysen's congregation may have added unction to the good Dutchman's testimony against formalism as embodied in the person of the visionary minister of Freehold.[36]

In the first constitutional debates in the Synod in 1721, Mr. Morgan, along with Jonathan Dickinson, took the position of dissent from Synod's supremacy and authority in framing acts of discipline and government which should have coercive force upon "subordinate judicatories."

The following year the dissidents, while acknowledging the power of the keys, and the authority of Synod in matters of appeal, yet hold, with the apparently unanimous endorsement of the Synod, the position that "Synods may compose directories and recommend them to all their members, respecting all the parts of discipline, provided that all subordinate judicatories may decline from such directories when they conscientiously think they have just cause to do so.' This remarkable compromise was hailed with acclamations of thanksgiving and praise, and was considered the solution of the relation of the Courts of the Church.

In the more important debate of 1729, on the Adoption of the Westminster standards, Mr. Morgan was absent although "timeous notice thereof" was given. The troubles in his own congregation which had culminated in the grave and varied charges brought against him, by some in the congregation led to his separation from the Presbyterian church of Freehold in the year 1729 or 1730.

These charges were before the Synod of 1728, presumably on an appeal from the Presbytery of Philadelphia. They were seven in number. On the first three he is sustained; Synod holding on the third, that "the accusers had no just ground for separation on that score." The fourth accusation is the curious charge of Mr. Morgan's practice of the art of astrology. The actions complained of had been performed in the earlier part of his ministry at Freehold, in the days of his navigation schemes, for his accusers have "partook with him in sealing ordinances many years after the things were done they complain of." Nevertheless, Synod finds more in this charge than in the others and "cannot clear Mr. Morgan from imprudence and misconduct in making the two alleged experiments of that kind, if the reports be true, were his ends never so good and laudable." The "two alleged experiments" are unfortunately mentioned no further.

"As to the fifth article, although the Synod do not approve promiscuous dancing, yet they judge it a clear indication of the captious and querulous spirit of Mr. Morgan's accusers, that they offer such a complaint against him." This is taken by many to mean Mr. Morgan's "countenancing" dancing.

The last charge is the unfortunate one of intemperance, which the Synod holds to be groundless. The Synod three years later, (1731) elected him Moderator, as though to show their confidence in him. Mr. Morgan's subsequent troubles when connected with the Churches of Hopewell and Maidenhead, have been held by many to have been caused by intemperance also, although there is no mention of the cause in the censure and suspension, for a time, on account of "gross scandals" and "repeated miscarriages."

Dr. McLean, in his lecture on Joseph Morgan, says that "as there was no hope of his promoting peace and union or of his being farther useful he resigned his charge." His last connection with the Presbyterians is contained in the records of the Tennent Church.

<blockquote>October 15th, 1730. The Revd. Mr. Joseph Morgan [having made a complaint against this congregation that they owed him above 200 pounds arrears of Sallerie] met the congregation at the Old Scots meeting House, where accompts were fairly made up, and Mr. Morgan gave the congregation a Discharge in full."[37]</blockquote>

His last scenes with the Dutch congregation were more agreeable. He remained with them until 1731, preaching his farewell sermon on August 31, when the short period of John Tennent's active ministry in the Presbyterian Church was nearly ended.

The Consistory of the Dutch church gave him at his departure a testimony of their appreciation of his services. They declare him to be a man of "acknowledged orthodoxy and exemplary character who, according to his ability, has faithfully and zealously performed the duties of his charge."[38]

He was far from being inactive as a missionary in the destitute parts of the county. At Allentown he preached, in his earlier ministry with the Freehold church, and wrote to Mather of meeting there with a cold reception. Later, in 1721, he writes more cheerfully of the changed attitude of that community toward Presbyterian ministers. In 1722, a church having been built at Allentown, Morgan was instrumental in securing Rev. Mr. Walton, a Yale graduate, as its minister.[39]

At Middletown, also, Mr. Morgan preached in a building which, even in his day, was dilapidated and left to decay. Its neglected condition annoyed him, and when riding by, if he saw the door or window open, he would stop, and dismounting his horse, reverently close the open door or window before proceeding on his way.[40]

At Shrewsbury also was a Presbyterian house of worship for his services in 1727.[41]

The dissatisfaction with his ministry followed him to his field of Hopewell and Maidenhead, resulting in the further charges already mentioned. The secret of his failure, with its salutary lesson may be learned from his own words "While free from worldly avocations, the work of grace went on abundantly, and people came from every quarter to receive spiritual consolation. It would even melt one's heart to see the humiliation, self-abasement, and self-loathing, that appeared in them; and then fleeing to the blood of Christ for relief, and to the free grace and good pleasure of God, to draw them to Christ, and to see the change wrought in their lovely souls." But, he continues, "when from necessity he [the minister] entangles himself in the affairs of this life the scene was mournfully changed."[42] Poor Morgan with his strange vagaries, and noble ideas, and moments of fervor, and times of temptation and abasement, a sweet but sad character, lovable and pitiable, as well.

Beautiful, and true we trust, is the tradition concerning his later days; that under the fiery impulse of Whitefield's eloquence, the spirit of Evangelism seized him in the rapture of a noble effort, and he traversed the sea coasts of New Jersey, proclaiming the Gospel in desolate places; and dying in the ardor of his aftermath, rests in an unknown grave.[43]

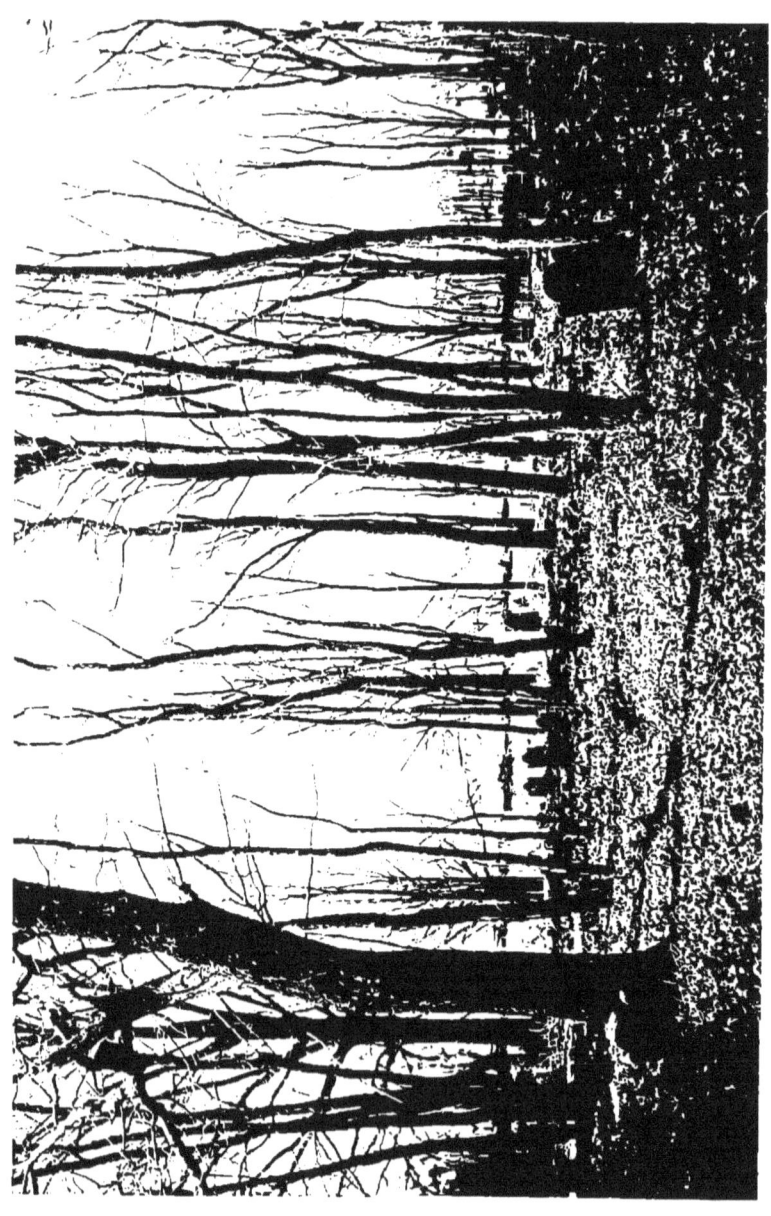

The "Old Scots" Burying Ground Looking Southwest. The Grave of Rev. John Tennent to the Right of the Background.

CHAPTER VI.

REV. JOHN TENNENT.

His Early Life, Conversion, Training, Licensure. Condition of The Freehold Church. Walter Ker's Effort. The Ordination. His Ministry and Success. His Death. His Tombstone. His Writings. Summary of His Life.

From the scenes of discord and contention in the later years of the unfruitful ministry of Morgan, it is with a sense of glad relief that we turn to the character and labor of the succeeding pastor, the Rev. John Tennent, who in the short period of his service with the church effected a spiritual work which was not only one of deep and lasting benefit to the congregation of Freehold, but was the harbinger and first fruits of the wonderful era of " The Great Awakening."

Rev. John Tennent was the third son of Rev. William Tennent, the founder of the " Log College," and the younger brother of Rev. Gilbert Tennent and Rev. William Tennent, jr.; the latter succeeding him in the ministry at Freehold. He was born in county Armagh, Ireland, November 12th, 1707, the year after his father had been ordained to the priesthood of the Established Church by the Bishop of Down.[44] In his eleventh year he came with his father and brothers to America, his oldest brother, Gilbert, being converted while on shipboard. The same year, dissenting from the orders, discipline, and false doctrines connived at in the Irish established church, Rev. Mr. Tennent, sr., was received into membership by the " Reverend Synod, held at Philadelphia, the 17th day of September. 1718." Mr. Tennent preached at Eastchester, Bedford, and other places in Westchester county, N.Y.,[45] following Morgan's labors on the same fields twenty years before, until, in 1726, he removed to the historic spot at Neshaminy, Penn., that will ever be connected with his name and fame. In the rude "Log College," the school of the prophets of the Revival days, he trained his four sons for the gospel ministry, and provided many other candidates for the sacred calling with such practical and spiritual equipment for service, that the impress of his personality, and the work of his pupils were dominant factors in the Presbyterianism of the succeeding generation.

Apart from his share in the changes in his father's life, little is known of the early days of John Tennent. An account of his conversion, which occurred in his youth, was published after his death by his brother Gilbert. His convictions were exceedingly deep and pungent, being terrible for the space of four days and nights, after which, being enabled to embrace Christ. his joys and consolations were as remarkable, as had been his anguish and sorrow on account of his sin.

After his education at the "Log College," he was licensed to preach by the Presbytery of New Castle, September, 18th, 1729, subscribing to the following declaration:

"I do own the Westminster Confession of Faith, before God and these witnesses, together with the Larger and Shorter Catechisms, with the Directory thereto annexed, to be the confession of my faith, and rule of faith and manners, according to the word of God."[46]

On the following day, the Synod of Philadelphia passed the important "Adopting Act," approving the Westminster standards "as being in all the essential and necessary articles, good forms of sound words and systems of Christian doctrine." Mr. John Tennent began his work as a preacher as a supply at Brandywine, Middletown, New Castle, and Middle and Lower Octorara.

The Freehold church, at the time of the retirement of Rev. Joseph Morgan, was in a deplorable condition. In a letter to Rev. Thomas Prince, of Boston, dated Oct. 11th, 1744, William Tennent, jr., drew the following picture of the state of the church: "The major part of the congregation could not be said to have so much as a name to live. Family prayer was unpractised by all, a very few excepted. Ignorance so overshadowed their minds, that the doctrine of the new birth, when clearly explained and powerfully pressed upon them, as absolutely necessary to salvation [by that faithful preacher of God's word, Mr. Theodorus Jacobus Frelinghuysen, a low Dutch minister, and some other English ministers, who were occasionally here] was made a common game of, so that not only the preachers but professors of that truth were called, in derision, "New born," and looked upon as holders forth of some new and false doctrine; and indeed their practice was as bad as their principles, viz.: "loose and profane."[47] This statement, with its careful exclusion of reference to Mr. Morgan and his preaching, gives a painful view of the result of his ministry. Coldness and unfruitfulness were however by no means qualities peculiar to the Freehold church in that period. It was a generation of skepticism, of formalism and of ecclesiastical controversies. Morgan's preaching and ministry was but the reflection of the condition of the church throughout the colonies and in Great Britain.[48]

Mr. Tennent further said to Mr. Prince, "In this miserable, hopeless, and helpless condition they lay, and few among them had either eyes to see or hearts to bewail their woful and wretched circumstances." A statement probably sufficiently strong to cover the facts. He adds, significantly that the people "were so divided among themselves, that it appeared improbable they would ever agree in the settlement of another Pastor." The dry, bookish, controversial essays of Morgan, on Predestination, or Baptism, with possibly veiled allusions to Astrology or water engines, surely were not calculated to renew the hearts of his hearers, and would also tend to cause the division in the congregation which was intimated in the answer of Synod to the charges preferred against Mr. Morgan in 1728. Other indications of a division among the people may be noted in the application for the granting of a permit, under George I, in 1727, for the erection of a new church upon "White Hill," which resulted in the present "Tennent" church building. The fact that the deed for the possession of the "Old Scots" ground was obtained in this same year, 1727, would seem to show the existence of two parties, one favoring the retention of the church at the former site, the other, the firmer Scotch party, headed by Ker, Craig and Rhea, proposing to remove to the western position, about which many of the sturdiest Scotch settlers had already clustered in their plantations.

At this critical time in the church's history, distressed at the contentions and seeking a pastor who might heal them, Walter Ker left his farm in the midst of harvest, and journeyed to Neshaminy, to endeavor to persuade Mr. John Tennent to return with him immediately and take charge of the congregation. At first Mr. Tennent positively refused even to visit Freehold. Mr. Ker, leaving him with sadness, told him with much solemnity, that he felt sure Mr. Tennent would soon come to a very different conclusion. Scarcely had Mr. Ker left when Mr. Tennent sent after him, saying he would come. It is said that the congregation, interested in Mr. Ker's mission, gathered in his crops for him, and the following year, amid wide-spread blasting and loss, Ker was able to provide seed for many who were destitute.

Even after Mr. Tennent had made this promise he expressed to his brother William's great regret that he had consented even to visit a people who seemed to be given up of God for their abuse of privileges. On his first visit to Freehold, probably in the close of the year 1729, he remained only four or five Sabbaths, but his preaching was so blessed in awakening and arousing the people, that on his return home, he told his brother that he was persuaded Christ had a large harvest of souls to be gathered in Freehold, and that though they were a poor, broken, divided people, yet if they called him, he would go though he should be obliged to beg his bread.[49]

The earliest records of the Tennent church now extant are minutes of congregational actions in the year 1730. After agreeing as to site of the new meeting house, it is voted " also that the Revd. Mr. John Tennent year Begin the 15th day of April last past, viz., 1730."

Seven months later Mr. Tennent was ordained as may be seen from the following extract from the records of the Tennent church.

"A true copy by me, John Henderson, Clerk, Tuesday, November 19th, 1730. There the Presbytry, or a committee of the same, met at the Scots Meeting house, and after fasting and prayer, and strict examination and full approbation, Did ordain the Rev. Mr. John Tennent. The Ministerial charge in [to?] this congregation, William Tennent, Jonethan Dickinson, Joseph Morgan and Gilbert Tennent. The names of the committee for the congregation was Walter Kerr, Robert Cumming, John Henderson, Robert Newell, —— Wilson, George Walker, Timothy Lloyde and Charles Gordon."[50]

The ministry of John Tennent was attended from the first with extraordinary tokens of divine power. "The place of worship," wrote his brother William to Mr. Prince, "was usually crowded with people of all ranks and orders, as well as professions, and they seemed to hear generally as for their lives. A solemn awe of God's majesty possessed many so that they behaved themselves as at his bar, while in his house. Many tears were usually shed when he preached, and sometimes the body of the congregation was moved and affected. I can say, and let the Lord alone have the glory of it, that I have seen both minister and people wet with their tears as with a bedewing rain. It was no uncommon thing to see persons, in the time of hearing, sobbing as if their hearts would break, but without any public outcry; and some have been carried out of the assembly, [being overcome] as if they had been dead."

This brief and brilliant ministry of John Tennent at Freehold was as the morning star of the dawning spiritual light that was now to spread throughout the church of America and England. While he was preaching with such intensity of awakening power, Whitefield was a lad in his mother's tavern at Gloucester and the "Holy Club" at Oxford was just being formed. Edwards did not until five years later see the effect of his tremendous proclamations upon the awe-struck audi-

The Pulpit of the Tennent Church, from which the Tennents, Whitefield, Brainerd, and Woodhull Preached. In the Square Enclosure Before the Pulpit Brainerd's Indian Converts Communed.

ences at Northampton, and not until seven years after John Tennent's death did John Wesley follow Whitefield's bold lead in the practice of the open-air preaching which was the actual beginning of the English revivals. "The earliest manifestation of the presence of the Holy Spirit, in our portion of the church, during this period, was at Freehold, N. J., under the ministry of the Rev. John Tennent."[51]

Under the ardor of his intense and emotional labors his strength was quickly exhausted, and within one year from the time of his ordination he was unable longer to proclaim the message of the gospel to which he devoted all the energy of his enthusiastic and consecrated life. Calling for his brother William's assistance in the work among a congregation which was rapidly increasing and needing most constant oversight, John Tennent lingered through the winter of 1730-31, in a state of happiness and peace, which turned into glowing ecstacy before his death. "A few moments before he expired," said his brother Gilbert, "he broke out in the following rapturous expressions: 'Farewell my brother—farewell father and mother—farewell world, with all thy vain delights—welcome God of father—welcome sweet Lord Jesus—welcome death, welcome eternity—Amen.' In a low voice he added, 'Lord Jesus, come Lord Jesus,' and so he fell asleep in Christ."

In the Tennent church record is this simple and affecting statement:

"Lord's day, April 23, 1732. The Revd. & Dear Mr. John Tennent Departed this Life between 8 & 9 of the clock in The morning, and was Burried on The Tuesday following, a mournful Providence & cause of great Humility To This poor congregation, To be bereaved of the flour of youth, The most Laborious, successful, well qualifide Pastor This age aforeded, Tho but a youth of 24 years, 5 months & 11 days of age."

His remains lie in the "Old Scots" graveyard, about eight paces southwest of John Boyd's stone. A sandstone tablet, some six feet by three, in a perfect state of preservation, lies flat above the grave, sinking already in the yielding turf. Upon it is an inscription prepared, it is said, by Jonathan Dickinson; and though there be little poetic merit in the epitaph, it shows the estimate placed on Mr. Tennent by one of the leading men of the age in which he lived. The inscription is as follows:

> Here lyes what was mortal of
> the Revrd, Mr. JOHN TENNENT
> Nat, Nou. 12. 1707 Obijt April 23
> 1732
>
> Who quick grew old in Learning Vertue Grace
> Quick finish'd well yielded to Deaths Embrace
> Whose mouldred Dust this Cabinet contains
> Whose soul triumphant with bright Seraph reigns
> Waiting the time all Heaven bright Concave flame
> And yⁱ last Trump repairs this rund Frame
> Cur praematuram mortemque queram acerbam
> Mors matura venit cum bona Vita fuit.

The only productions we have from the pen of John Tennent are the two sermons published in London by his brother Gilbert "with an explanatory Address to Saints and Sinners." The sermons are on "The Nature of Regeneration opened and its absolute Necessity in order to Salvation demonstrated," and on "The Nature of Adoption with its consequent Privileges explained."

"From these sermons and from the testimony of both his brothers, Gilbert and William, and from the accounts which have come down to us, and especially from the extraordinary success which attended his brief ministry, we have every reason to conclude, that in piety, talents, and preaching ability, he was quite equal to either of his brothers, and probably, as a preacher, superior to either of them; and had he lived would probably have surpassed either of them in his usefulness to the Church of God. According to tradition his zeal was ardent, his style beautiful, with a remarkable fluency of expression, and luxuriance and aptness of illustration, while a peculiar tenderness, compassion, and pathos, breathed in all he said, even while denouncing the terrors of the law against the secure and impenitent. The people of his charge were greatly attached to him, and deeply mourned and lamented his death; and his memory is even yet fragrant in Freehold, among the descendants of those who sat under his ministry."

CHAPTER VII.

THE REMOVAL OF THE CHURCH.

Reasons for the Removal. Fear of Division. Change in Location of Settlers. Decay of The "Old Scots" Meeting-House. William Tennent, Jr. John Woodhull, D. D. Walter Ker's Grave.

The first motion looking to the removal of the church was the permit from the Crown for the proposed building, obtained in 1727.[52] In 1728, on some unknown charge against Mr. Morgan, Synod finds his accusers have "no just ground for separation." In 1730, on July 20th, the elders, Walter Ker and John Hutton,[53] with their "helps" who are "to represent the congregation," Charles Gordon, Timothy Lloyde, Jonithan Forman, Robert Cumming, and John Henderson,[54] met and "agreed to build a meeting-House between Wm. Ker's Barrs and Rockey Hill Bridge."

Three reasons for this new building may be deduced from the records. First, there was clearly an apprehension of a division in the congregation, and the consistent, Scotch element in the church, led by Walter Ker, who had always been out of sympathy with Mr. Morgan, wished to prepare for the possible separation, by providing a place for the accomodation of the large portion who were disaffected at the close of Mr. Morgan's ministry. Second, there appears to have been a change in the location of many of the Presbyterian settlers in the early years of the century. The strongest supporters of the church were on plantations several miles west of

The Tennent Church. Built 1730, Enlarged 1753.

the "Old Church;" the newer Scotch element, coming over in the time of the Jacobite troubles of 1715, found the eastern portion of the county already pre-empted, and went where Proprietor's land could be obtained; the Dutch had also entrenched themselves gregariously about the former site. Thirdly, the earlier building had evidently been of such a rude and temporary character, that there was need of a new church, on the old site or elsewhere. A fortnight after the above-mentioned meeting of the representatives of the church, they agreed "that the Old or lower meeting-House To be repaired with all Haste that can be."

Managers, or "undertakers," in building the new church were appointed in August, 1730, between the call and the ordination of John Tennent. The new church "is to be made Forty feet long and Thirty feet wide, and each of the Builders is to have one seat in it above their common Due."

The work which was to be pushed "with all the speed possible after this sowing time was over," was successfully advanced in the winter, and on "April 18th, 1731, was The first Time that there was servise in the new meeting-House on White Hill." On the same day Margaret, daughter of William Ker was baptized, "the first Baptized in the new Meeting House."

A tradition has been handed down that it was planned by the "undertakers" to locate the church upon a site lower than its present situation, and that old Janet Rhea,[55] one of the Scotch Covenanters, seized the small corner-stone in her apron, and toiling to the top of the hill, set it upon the summit, saying to the astonished builders, "Wha ever heard o' ganging doon to the Hoose o' the Lord, an no o' ganging oop to the Hoose o' the Lord?" A fine mixture of aspiration and scripture literalness, characteristic of Covenanter stock. The agreement was made in 1730, "That the services be one Sabbath at the upper Meeting House, and so to continue successively," which apparently meant alternate services at the "Scots" church and the "Tennent" church. About the year 1733, under the ministry of Rev. William Tennent, jr., services were held for two Sabbaths in the new church, and one in the old church. In course of time, from the decay of the slight structure reared in the first days of the new settlement, and from the superior accommodations and more convenient situation of the newer church, the "Old Scots Meeting-House," on Free Hill, crumbled, fell and passed into oblivion so utterly, that no tradition remains of its size, appearance, or appurtenances.

Concerning the famed ministry of Rev. William Tennent, jr., in the church and community that bears his name and cherishes his memory, little may properly be said within the limits of the present subject. His energy and apostolic zeal, his shrewdness, wit, and consecrated sense, his prodigious labors, and the accounts, well-nigh miraculous, of supernatural acts and scenes, are treasured thoughts and household tales in the broad region where he toiled with such success.

His body was buried in the central aisle of the church whose walls rang so often with the ardor of his eloquence. Before his year-old grave, Washington rallied the retreating Continental troops, upon that heated Sabbath day, in June, 1778, when brazen cannon lips thundered from Tennent heights the stern message of Liberty; and the dark menace of invasion rolled back from the little church front, where Strength and Conscience, Valor and Religion joined to repel the foe from Monmouth field.

Rev. John Woodhull, D. D., followed with an illustrious ministry of forty-five years, exerting a wide and benignant influence. Boyd, the Tennents, and Woodhull, four of the first five ministers, died while in their service with the church of Freehold.

Some half a mile eastward of the Tennent church, upon a thickly wooded hill, o'ergrown with tangled briars, that clamber over fallen trunks, on a point that looks out toward the white church he loved and toiled for through long years, lies the body of that man of God, Walter Ker. His tombstone is of firm-grained sandstone, with clear-cut inscription that reads as follows:

> Here lies what's Mortal of Walter Ker
> Deceased June 10th 1748 in ye 92 year of his age
> Who long with Patience Bore life's heavy load
> Willing to spend and be spent for God
> the noble Portrait in a line to paint
> he Breath'd, a Father liv'd,' & Dy'd a saint
> Here sleeps in peace the aged sire's dust
> Till the glad Trump arouse the sleeping just.

Beside him lies his wife, who had died fourteen years before. Above the little plot stands a massive oak with wide, strong branches which have resisted many a wintry shock, whose iron strength, deep rooted in the soil beneath, and lofty in its grand, uplifted limbs, seems as a type of that noble Covenanter's soul, who, after suffering imprisonment for conscience sake, banished across the sea, prayed and toiled and sacrificed, through three score years, for the Church of the Eternal Covenant of God. Beside the oak stands a strong and graceful chestnut tree, and the two, with branches intertwined, are symbols of those true and upright lives, rooted in the certainty of the promises of God, and sublime in the aspirations for the heavenly life. Down below the eminence where the trees are shading the ancient graves, rolls a fertile field and on its grassy sward, under fruit-laden branches, graze flocks of sheep and herds of placid cattle.

From the rugged grandeur of those stern, strong, God-fearing lives of the troublous past, descend to our more peaceful days the inspiration of noble inheritance, and the treasured memories of the lineage of God's elect.

> "Peace to the Church, her peace no foes invade;
> Peace to each noble martyr's noble shade,
> They with undaunted courage, truth, and zeal,
> Contended for the Church and Country's weal.
> We share the fruits, we drop the grateful tear,
> And peaceful altars o'er their ashes rear."

FINIS.

APPENDIX.

1. Margaret Wilson was but eighteen years of age. Her epitaph in the church yard at Wigton reads:

> "Murdered for owning Christ supreme
> Head of his church, and no more crime,
> But her not owning Prelacy,
> And not abjuring Presbytery,
> Within the sea, tied to a stake,
> She suffered for Christ Jesus' sake."
> [See Macaulay, Hist. of England i. 379.]

2. The list is given in W. A. Whitehead's Contributions to the Early History of Perth Amboy, etc., p. 22. In this list we find the name of John Craige, probably he who in 1705 headed the number of those who applied to the Monmouth county court to have the Presbyterian meeting house on Freehill recorded; of Archibald Craige, who was his son, and who with two children lies buried in the "Old Scots" ground; of John Boyd perhaps some connection of the John Boyd, who 21 years later was minister of the church at Freehold.

3. In 1684, Gawen Lawrie, Deputy Governor of East Jersey, wrote "The Scots and William Dockwra's people coming now and settling advanced the Province more than it hath been advanced these ten years." Again he writes: "The Scots have taken a right course. They have sent over many servants and are likewise sending more. They have likewise sent over many poor families and given them a small stock." William Dockwra was a London merchant, inventor of the Penny Post. He was said to be in 1688 "the best land stead in the Province." [See N. J. Archives 11. 27.] John Reid, who became Surveyor General of the Province, and of His Majesty's council, came in 1683 in charge of one of Barclay's expeditions. He was a Quaker, turning in 1702 to the English church under Keith's influence. He lies buried about two miles from the "Old Scots" ground, in Topanemus graveyard. [See Ellis' History of Monmouth County p. 79.]

4. The "Caledonia" has been the centre of much romance, and possibly some mythology, voiced in the expression of an old negro woman of Perth Amboy, "that Ham and Columbo came over in the old Caledonia. A ship of that name was one of the five of the unfortunate Scotch expedition to Darien in 1698, and one of the three that came after the disastrous termination of the venture, to New York in the autumn of 1699.

Macaulay, [v:177] says: "The Caledonia, the healthiest ship of the three, threw overboard a hundred corpses." It is known that one of her sister ships from Darien, the "Unicorn," came to Amboy, under the command of John Anderson, a "Scotch Presbyterian," [See N. J. Archives, vol iv., pp. 156, 178] who lies buried at Topanemus, two miles from the "Old Scots" ground. Whitehead, [Contribution to History of Perth Amboy, etc. pp. 265, 266] says that the "Caledonia" brought over many Scotch families in 1715, and that the remains of the vessel could be seen in recent years in shoal water off Amboy. It is said that in the latter part of the last century the broken mast of the vessel was a familiar sight. Canes and other articles made from her timbers are still preserved.

5. Walter Ker came from the Parish of Dalsert, Lanarkshire, and was banished two days before Pitlochie's expedition sailed through the influence of the curate of the Parish, Joseph Clelland.

William Tennent, Jr., in 1744, wrote concerning Freehold: "The settling of that place with a gospel ministry, was owing, under God, to the agency of some Scotch people, that came to it, among whom there was none so painstaking in this blessed work as one Walter Ker, who, in 1685, for his faithful and conscientious adherence to God and his truth as professed by the church of Scotland, was there apprehended and sent to this country, under a sentence of perpetual banishment. By which it appears that the devil and his instruments lost their aim in sending him from home, where it is unlikely he could ever have been so serviceable to Christ's kingdom as he has been here He is yet [1744] alive; and, blessed be God, flourishing in his old age, being in his 88th year." [See Hodge's History, part ii., p. 20.]

Salter's History of Monmouth and Ocean counties,[Appendix,page 1 xxvii,] states he was banished Sept. 3, 1685, was probably on the "Henry and Francis;" he had sons, Joseph and James, (perhaps William and Samuel also, who were deacons in the church in 1746). Walter Ker, with his wife, Margaret, and his son Joseph's wife, Margaret, lies buried about half a mile east of the present "Old Tennent" church.

Concerning one Walter Ker, the "sweet singer" of 1681, who can hardly have been the same, [see Wodrow, iii., pp. 348,353, and Whitehead, Contributions, etc. pp. 38, 40.]

6. [See Ellis' History of Monmouth County, p. 830]:—On a farm near Matawan is a broken and defaced stone partly illegible, bearing the words "Here lies interred the Body,""William Robertson,""Great Britian" and the date 1682. Tradition says "he came from Scotland in the famous prison ship and that it was he who named the place New Aberdeen."

7. Lewis Morris' letter to the Bishop of London in 1700 says: "Freehold was settled from Scotland [Mr. Keith began the first settlement there, and owned a fine plantation, which he afterwards sold, and went into Pennsylvania.] About one half of the inhabitants there are Scotch Presbyterians, and a sober people. The other part was settled by people [some from New England, some from New York, and some from the formentioned towns,] who are, generally speaking, of no religion. There is in this town a Quaker Meeting House." By this Morris means Topanemus which was afterwards moved to Freehold village, constituting part of the present edifice of St. Peter's church. It is to be noted that Morris does not mention the existence in 1700 of a Scotch Meeting House at Freehold. This is no proof of its nonexistence at that date, however, as Morris also ignores the Baptist Meeting house at Middletown, which had undoubtedly been built some twelve years before. [See "Old Times in Old Monmouth," p. 264.]

8. The ground lies seven-eighths of a mile west of the track of the Freehold and Atlantic Highlands Branch of the C. R. R. of N. J., about equidistant from Bradevelt and Wickatunk stations, on a straight road from the latter. It lies on the "John VanKirk farm," opposite the home of Mr. Gideon McDowell, and is about five miles northeast of the "Old Tennent" Church, its successor.

9 These dimensions would make the building larger than the famous "Log College," built over thirty years afterwards, where two of the preachers of the Freehold Church, John and William Tennent were trained by their father. [See Whitefield's Life, by Gillies, p. 61.]

10. The eighteen century stones in the grave yard are as follows:
Rev. John Boyd, died August 30th, 1708, aet. 28.
Michael Henderson, and Jane, his wife, died 1722.
William Redford, born 1642, died March 1725-6.

William Craig, son of Archibald, died Aug. 8, 1726, aet 1.
Margaret Redford, wife of William, born 1645, died 1729.
Rev. John Tennent, born Nov. 12 1707, died April 23, 1732.
Richard Clark, born in Scotland Feb 10th, 1663, died May 16, 1733.
Elinor, wife of Abraham VanDorn, daug. of Jonathan and Margaret Forman, died May 22, 1733, aet. 20.
William, son of Jonathan and Margaret Forman, born Feb. 20, 1729, died 1735.
Elizabeth, wife of Jeremiah Reeder, died 1735, aet. 79.
Stevens Nicholas Henderson, grandson of Michael Henderson, died Nov. 27 1737, 9 month old
Walter Wall, died Feb. 2, 1737-8, aet 47.
William, son of Samuel Craig, died Aug. 23, 1743, aet. 2.
Catharine, wife of John Vanderhiden, daug. of Anthony and Elizabeth Ward, died Jan. 10, 1746, aet. 33.
Samuel, son of Archibald Craig, died Nov. 17, 1746, aet. 38.
Anthony Ward, born Great Britain, died Dec. 6, 1746, aet. 76.
Euphemia Freeiser, died Mar. 1, 1747-8 aet. 21.
Anne Henderson, born Dec. 27, 1734, died June 18, 1748.
Samuel Crawford, died July 8, 1748, aet. 35 years, 3 months.
Jane Henderson, born Oct. 8, 1730, died Jan. 4, 1748-9.
Archibald Craig, Esq., died Mar. 6, 1751, aet. 73.
Mary, wife of Archibald Craig, died Nov. 1, 1752, aet. 69.
Anna, wife of Walter Wall, died Jan. 19, 1758, aet. 62 and about 4 months.
Jonathan, son of Jonathan and Margaret Forman, born Nov. 13, 1722, died May 20, 1758
William Crawford, died Mar. 22, 1760, aet. 49.
Margaret, daug. of John and Sarah O'Harrah, died Sep. 3, 1760, aet. 5.
John O'Harrah, died Sep. 16, 1760, aet. 34.
Hannah, wife of John Amy, died Mar. 23, 1762, aet. about 53.
Jonathan Forman, died Dec. 28, 1762, aet. 74.
Margaret, widow of Jonathan Forman, born 1693, died Dec. 21, 1765.
John Henderson, died Jan. 1, 1771, aet. 73.
Catharine, wife of John Patten, died Feb. 9, 1774, aet. 52.
Anne, wife of John Henderson, died Oct. 4, 1776, aet. 64.
David Pease, died Oct. 15, 1778, aet. 58.

In several cases the husband and wife, or the parent and child or grandchild lie beneath the same stone.

11. The earliest date in the existing records of the Freehold Church is 1730. Many of the old records were lost in the burning of the parsonage of Rev. Archibald Cobb, pastor of the Tennent church. The accounts extant assume a regular organization already existing. With their orderly Scotch habits, the appointment of elders, or "Assistants" was an early act. In the neighboring church of Woodbridge, in 1707, 1708 "the foundation of the church was laid first upon three persons who had been communicants, etc." [Whitehead's Contributions, p. 386.]

In "a sermon preached at Freehold Nov. 25, 1824, on the death of the Rev. John Woodhull, D. D., late pastor of the Presbyterian church of Freehold, New Jersey, by the Rev. Isaac N. Brown" (p. 25, note) it is stated. "This congregation was regularly organized June 3, 1730. Before this it had nominally existed a short time and enjoyed the pastoral labors of the Rev. Joseph Morgan." An account ignoring John Boyd may not be considered conclusive.

12. In Scot's "Model, etc." Peter Watson's letter from E. Jersey, of Aug. 20, 1684, says "We have great need of good and faithful ministers, and I wish to God, that there would some come over here, they can live as well

and have as much as in Scotland, and more than many get; we have none within all the province of East Jersey except one who is preacher in Newark; there were one or two preachers more in the Province, but they are dead, and now the people they meet together every Sabbath day, and read and pray, and sing Psalms in their meeting-houses."

13. In the Monmouth Patent of 1665, religious toleration was provided for: "They shall have free liberty of conscience without any molestation or disturbance whatsoever in their way of worship." But the force and authority of the Patent was an uncertain quantity. Cornbury's Instructions from the Crown (1702) provided for "Liberty of conscience to all persons except Papists." [N. J. Archives, ii. 522.]

Scot in his "Model" 1684, says: "Liberty in matters of religion is established in the fullest manner. To be a planter or inhabitant, nothing is required but the acknowledging of one Almighty God; and to have a share in the government, a simple profession of faith of Jesus Christ without descending into any other of the differences among Christians, only that religion may not be a cloak for disturbance, whoever comes into the magistrature, must declare they hold not themselves in conscience obliged for religion's sake to make an alteration or to endeavor to turn out their partners to the government because they differ in opinion with them; and this is no more than to follow the great rule, to do as they would be done by."

14. See reply of Assembly of 1707 to Cornbury, [N. J. Archives, iii. 264.] "One minister of the church of England, dragg'd by a sheriff from Burlington to Amboy, and there kept in custody, without assigning any reason for it, and at last haul'd by force into a boat by your excellency, and transported like a malefactor into another government, and there kept in garrison as a prisoner; and no reason assigned for these violent procedures, but your excellency's pleasure. Another minister of the Church of England, laid under a necessity of leaving the province from the reasonable apprehensions of meeting the same treatment, etc."

In Cornbury's Instructions from the Crown he was directed not "to prefer any minister to an ecclesiastical benefice without a certificate from the Right Reverend Father in God, the Bishop of London, of his being conformable to the doctrine and discipline of the Church of England." He was also directed to remove such as give scandals by their doctrine or morals, a dangerous power to place in the hands of a governor with the doctrines and morals of Cornbury. [See N. J. Archives, ii. p. 528.]

15. "Court of Quarter Sessions, held at Shrewsbury, May 28th, 1706.

Whereas, Mr. John Boyd, Minister of ye Presbyterians of Freehold, made application to ye Court of Sessions, held last December, that he might be admitted to qualifie himself, as ye law directs in that behalf and ye Court ordered that further consideration thereof should be referred. And now ye said John Boyd appeared in open session, and was by the court permitted to qualifie himself, and accordingly the said John Boyd hath qualified himself as ye law in that case directs, viz: did take ye oath made, in a statute, made in the first year of their Majesties Reign, entitled, "An act for removing and preventing all questions and disputes concerning ye assembling of ye Parliament; and did make and subscribe ye declaration mentioned in ye statute made in ye 30th year of ye reign of King Charles ye 2nd, intitled, 'An act to prevent Papists from sitting in either house of Parliament,' and did also declare his approbation of, and did subscribe ye articles of religion mentioned in ye statute made in ye 30th year of the Reign of ye late Queen Elizabeth except ye 34, 35 and 36, and these words of ye 20th article, viz: "The Church hath power to decree rites or ceremonys and authority in controversies of faith and, etc.'

All which are entered here of record, according to ye directions of another Act of Parliament, entitled, "An act exempting his Majesties Protestant subjects, desenting from ye Church of England, from the penalties of certain laws."

"The Five Mile Act had banished him from his dwelling, from his relations, from his friends, from almost all places of public resort. Under the Conventicle Act his goods had been distrained, and he had been flung into one noisome goal after another among highwaymen and house breakers." Macaulay, Hist. II. 163.

See "Proceedings of Deputation to Protect civil rights of Dissenters." London, 1813, p. 172.

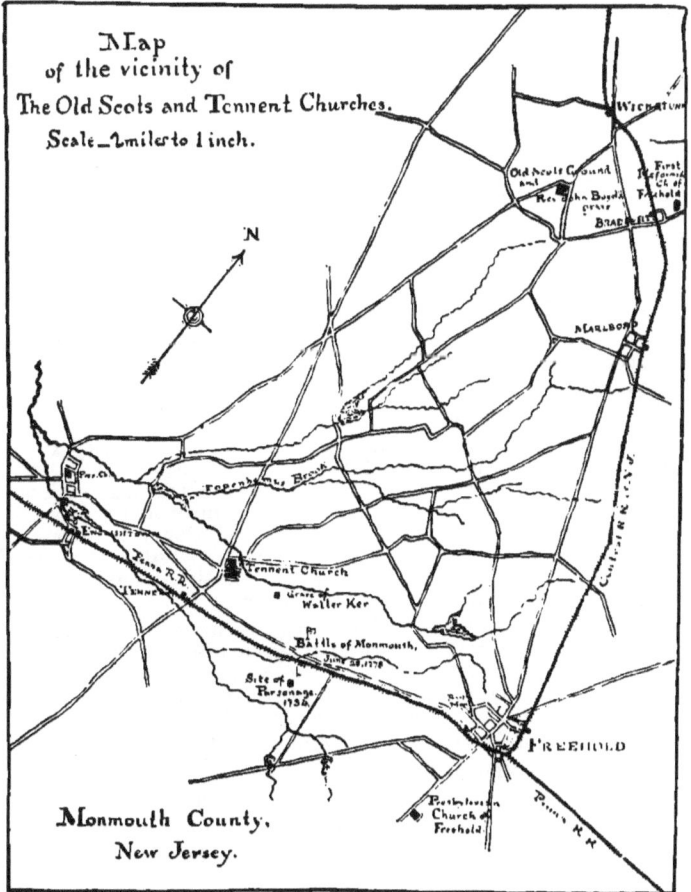

16. Rev. Mr. Talbot, of the S. P. G., wrote to its secretary in 1703, from Philadelphia [?]. "The Presbyterians here come a great way to lay hands on one another, but after all I think they had as good stay at home for all the good they do." See Gillett's History of Presb. Church, i, 20. In

"The Presb. Church in Philadelphia." [Introd., p. xiv.] it is said that Andrews was ordained and installed in 1701.

17. See Hodge's History, i. 78.

18. See Briggs' Amer. Presbyterianism, pp. 139 note, 140 note, and xliv.
Ten years later twelve of the seventeen in the Presbytery of Philadelphia were believed to have been educated at Glasgow. See "American Presbyterianism," App. p. lxxi.

19. See "Records of the Presbyterian Church," pp. 11, 12.

20. See History of Presb. Church of Trenton, by John Hall, D. D., p. 35. The Newark church was not connected with Presbytery till 1716-20. See J. F. Stearns' Hist. First Church of Newark," pp. 127, 128.

21. A John Boyd, in Ayrshire, Scotland, was schoolmaster at Cowend [Wodrow, iii. 385.] His house was thrice robbed of all its furniture by the soldiers, and he forced to pay 40 pounds to Ardmillan for failing to attend the curate's services. He was carried prisoner to Edinburgh in 1682 where he lay three months in close confinement, and before he was liberated, paid upwards of 100 pounds, Scots, whereby he was reduced to great wants.

The Rev. William Boyd, pastor of Lamington Presb. Church, 1784-1807, was "the son of John Boyd, a Scotch-Irishman, was born in Franklin county, Penn., where his father settled on removing to America." Manual of Lamington Church, p. 12. Mr. John Boyd VanDoren, of Princeton, considers Rev. Wm. Boyd "the son or direct descendant of the Rev. John Boyd of Monmouth."

An Adam Boyd appears in Synod in 1725. A John Boyd, at Upper Octorara, Penn., in 1736. A William Boyd came from Ireland to America on an inquiry about Scotch-Irish emigration in 1718.

22 See Note 18.

23. See Hodge's History, i. 78.

24. In an address on Rev. John Boyd before the Presbyterian Historical Society, delivered by Rev. D. V. McLean, D. D., it is said that Mr. Boyd "devoted some portion of his time to Middletown, preaching there at least as early as 1706." Dr. McLean holds that before the Scotch Immigration of 1682-5, Presbyterians from Connecticut and Long Island, settling in Monmouth county, "were active in establishing Presbyterian Congregations in Shrewsbury and Middletown where at least occasional services were held before they were in any other part of the county."

"The Presbyterian Church of Middletown had its commencement before 1706 and a church edifice was soon after erected on the old Presbyterian burying-ground lot." Ellis' Hist. Mon. Co., p. 532.

In Scot's "Model," 1684, speaking of the Independent churches of Middletown and Shrewsbury he says they "are most like Presbyterian."

25. See C. W. Baird's History of the Church in Bedford, N. Y.

26. See Mather's Magnalia, I. p. 88.

27. See Letter of Mr. Bartow's in Briggs Amer. Presbyterianism, p. 149.
Mr. Bartow married Helen, daughter of John Reid of Monmouth county. Their granddaughter, Theodosia, married Aaron Burr. Ellis' Hist. Mon. Co., p. 575.

28. Lecture before Presb. Hist. Soc. by D. V. McLean, D. D., on "Joseph Morgan." Other authorities hold the same.

29. See Hist. of Presb. Church of Trenton, p 46.

In a letter received from the Registrar of Yale College, F. B. Dexter, in 1889, it is stated of Joseph Morgan that "He was not a student here at any time, but received the honorary degree of Master of Arts about the year 1719; the exact date is not known.

30. See "Brick Church Memorial," by Rev. T. W. Wells, p. 22.

31. See "Brick Church Memorial," by Rev. T. W. Wells, p. 23.

32. Close connections existed in those early days between the Scotch and Dutch settlers. Two early graves in the "Old Scots" ground indicate by the "van," the marriages of Scotch daughters to the sons of Dutch immigrants. In 1714 Jonathan Forman united with the Dutch Church, a sufficient explanation of the fact being seen in his wife's maiden name of Wikof. This Forman was the fourth generation from Robert Forman, b. ab. 1610, in England, coming to Long Island in 1645, a connection, probably of the John Foreman, of the "Henry and Francis," who with John Frazer and five others, were seized in London, while hearing Rev. Alex Shields preach, cast into Newgate Prison, marched through London, manacled, two by two, sent to Scotland [indicating probably Scotch connection] examined by the Council, and sent to Dunnottar Castle. Webster's History Presbyterian Church, p. 70.

33. In the Library of the Conn. Hist. Society.

34. This, and his "Remedy for Mortal Errors," a sermon preached in 1723 on the death of his son Joseph, in which he "entertained" his audience with an account of "The duty and marks of Zion's children," and his last publication, a sermon on "Love to our neighbour commended," printed in Boston in 1749, may be found, (according to Dr. D. V. McLean) in the Antiquarian Society Library at Worcester, Mass Also his remarkable letter to Cotton Mather, quoted before. In this letter, written in Latin (of the day), he says "I spent only three years in the study of languages and the arts, and for twenty-five years I have labored almost constantly with my hands. A Latin, Greek, or Hebrew book I have sometimes not had in my hands for a whole year. I have scarcely any books; possess no dictionary but an imperfect Rider. I have no commentaries, nor theological systems nor histories." It is pleasant to learn that Mr. Mather furnished him soon with a library of useful books. D. V. McLean's Lecture on Joseph Morgan.

35. For this letter, full of quaintness, pedantry, garrulity, and noble sincerity, see Briggs' Amer. Presbyterianism, App. p. lxi.

36. See "Brick Church Memorial," p. 23.

37. See Ellis' Hist. of Mon. Co., p. 680.

38. See "Brick Church Memorial," p. 24.

39. See "Historical Discourse on Presb. Church of Allentown," by Geo. Swain, D. D., pp. 11, 12.

40. See Ellis' Hist. Mon. Co. p. 532 .

41. See Ellis' Hist. Mon Co. p. 584.

42. In his "Reply to an Anonymous Railer against the Doctrine of Election," repelling the slur on Presbyterian ministers for receiving a maintenance while preaching the Gospel.

43. See "Brick Church Memorial." p. 23.

44. See Webster's History, p. 364.

45. See C. W Baird's Hist Bedford Church, pp. 45, seq.

46. See Hodge's Hist. Presb Church, i. 88, note.

47. In Prince's Christian History, No. 91.

48. In 1721, Increase Mather wrote "There is a grievous decay of piety in the land, and a leaving of her first love ; a fruitful Christian grown too rare a spectacle."

In England, in 1736, Bishop Butler, wrote Christianity itself seemed to be regarded as a fable "among all persons of discernment."

49. For this incident, and many other facts concerning John Tennent, including the quoted paragraph at the close of the chapter, a debt of acknowledgment is owed to the Mss. Lectures of Dr. D. V. McLean. The Lecture on William Tennent, Jr., which passes beyond the scope of this work, is especially full and interesting.

50. These extracts from the earliest history recorded of the Church, are published in Ellis' Hist. of Mon. Co. pp. 680, 681.

51. Hodge's Hist. Presb. Church, ii., 20.

52. This "Perm't" was in existence some years ago, but seems to have disappeared, along with other valuable historical matter.

53. John Hutton had represented the Church at the Synods of 1727 and 1728, in the time of Morgan's troubles.

54. John Henderson's daughter Jane was "the first child ever the Rev. Mr John Tennent baptised." On her stone in the "Old Scots" ground is the inscription " Her Grace, Obedience, Good conduct and Grave sense caused Parents tears and neighbors observance."

55. Janet Rhea lies buried in a private plot of the Rhea family, on the D. D. Denise farm, one mile west of Freehold. The names and dates on the stones in the plot are as follows:
Janet Rhea. Died Jan. 15, 1761, aet. ab. 93.
Robert Rhe. Died Jan. 18, 1720.
David Rhea. Died May 15, 1761, aet. 64, and 2 months.
Jonathen Rhea, Died May 23, 1767, aet. 31 [or 91,] 9 months, and 1 day [This stone is broken into six fragments, making the age uncertain.]
Anna, daughter of Jonethan and Lydia Rhea, aet. 5 months.
Margreat, daughter of Robert and Mary Rhe. Died Nov. 10, 1747, aet. 1 year, 3 mos., 17 days.
David, son of Robert and Mary Rhe. Died Aug. 11, 1752, act 3 years 11 mos., 25 days
Margret, daughter of Robert & Mary Rhe. Died Aug. 16, 1752, aet. 1 year, 6 mos., 7 days.
In a family plot two miles east of Freehold, on "Wikoff's Hill" are the following headstones:—
Ursilla, wife of Aaron Forman Died Ap. 4, 1768, aet. 63
Aaron Forman, son of Sam'l. & Mary, Died Jan. 13, 1741-2, aet 42.
Samuel Forman, Died Oct. 13, 1740, aet 77.
Samuel Stelle, son of Ambrose and Rebekah Stelle. Died Oct. 16, 1721, aet. 2 years, 4 mos , 18 days.
Denise, son of John and Elinor Forman. Died Nov. 18, 1761, aet. 1 year 8 mos., 9 days
Mary, wife of Samuel Forman, died Mar. 18, 1728, aet. 61.
Eleanor Forman, daughter of John and Jane, died Oct. 18, 1730, aet. 3 years, and 7 mos.
Hannah Forman, daughter of John and Jane, died Sep. 30, 1730, aet. 15 mos.
Rebekah van Kleif, daughter of Samuel and Mary Forman, died Sep. 19, 1748, aet. 52.
Capt. John Forman, died Nov. 25, 1740, aet. 47 years, 2 mos., 2 days.
William Maddock, died Sep. 1, 1750, aet 59 years, 5 mos., 19 days.
Hannah, wife of William Maddock, died Jan. 11, 1755, aet. 65 years, 18 days.

There are some other old plots about Freehold, but the stones in them have either no inscriptions or are mostly undecipherable

The oldest stone in the Tennent yard is of Aaron Mattison, son of John and Elizabeth, 1744.

www.ingramcontent.com/pod-product-compliance
Lightning Source LLC
Chambersburg PA
CBHW022148090426
42742CB00010B/1430